WORKBOOK FOR MEN

$\int$AVING YOUR MARRIAGE BEFORE IT STARTS

———— EXPANDED & UPDATED EDITION ————

SEVEN QUESTIONS TO ASK BEFORE —AND AFTER—YOU MARRY

Drs. LES & LESLIE PARROTT

ZONDERVAN®

GRAND RAPIDS, MICHIGAN 49530 USA

ZONDERVAN.COM/
AUTHORTRACKER

ZONDERVAN®

Saving Your Marriage Before It Starts Workbook for Men
Copyright © 1995, 2006 by Les and Leslie Parrott
Expanded and Updated Edition

Requests for information should be addressed to:

Zondervan, *Grand Rapids, Michigan 49530*

ISBN-10: 0-310-26565-7
ISBN-13: 978-0-310-26565-8

Published in association with Yates & Yates, LLP, Attorneys and Counselors, Suite 1000, Literary Agent, Orange, CA.

Interior design by Beth Shagene

Printed in the United States of America

09 10 11 12 • 21 20 19 18 17 16 15 14 13 12 11 10

Contents

SESSIONS
For Group or Couple Discussion
with the DVD Curriculum

How to Use This Workbook

We have seen many couples who marry and then wait to see what will happen. This workbook is a tool to help you make the *right* things happen. Its brief exercises and activities, to be completed as you read through *Saving Your Marriage Before It Starts, Expanded and Updated Edition*, come from our work in counseling couples and are proven strategies for enriching and developing your relationship. Too often, reading a book can lead to great ideas, but little action. This workbook will help you put feet on the ideas and put them into action. And we believe you will enjoy it! As Shakespeare said, "Joy's soul lies in the doing." Before beginning, you may also want to take our premarital online assessment, which you can find at *www.RealRelationships.com*.

Why It's Ideal for Each of You to Have Your Own Workbook

This workbook is to be used in conjunction with your fiancée's (or wife's). There is one workbook designed for men and one for women, and it is important that each of you have your own copy. For the best results, each of you should work on the exercises separately, then meet together to discuss your answers. We know from working with countless couples that many of these exercises can serve as a potential epiphany for you—a real eye-opener—if you answer honestly (not trying to guess what your partner wants you to say).

This is why you'll get the most from these experiences if you each have your own copy of the workbook. In many places your answers would be influenced by seeing what your partner wrote and thus diminish the value of the exercise. In addition, the men's and women's workbooks are contextualized to each gender, and this one even has specific content for you as a man.

The Best Approach to These Exercises

While there is no one right way to use this workbook, we suggest that you complete the exercises as you encounter them in the book, or soon after you have finished reading the chapter that covers the exercise. In other words, try to complete the exercises for that chapter before moving on to the next one. The point is to integrate the exercises into the process of reading the book. Some of the exercises are designed to be used again and again, helping you continue to improve your communication, for example, or deepen your sense of intimacy. Others are more of a one-shot exercise and are exploratory in nature.

A Note about Wording

We've designed these exercises to be appropriate for you—whether you are seriously dating, engaged, or already married. So don't get hung up on the use of "husband/wife" if you aren't married yet. We've done our best to avoid awkward phrasing while still acknowledging your status. In some cases we may say "partner," for example, in order to include anyone who may be doing these exercises.

Using These Workbooks Long Distance

If you and your fiancée or spouse are not in close proximity at this time, you can still do these exercises together. In fact, we have heard from countless couples who are in the military or located in different cities for various reasons during their engagement period or early years of marriage, and they love doing these exercises long distance (over the phone or via email). They create a meaningful point of connection even when miles separate you.

As you work through the pages of this book, make it your own. Don't get too hung up on following the rules. If a particular exercise leads you down a more intriguing path, take it. Some of these exercises may simply serve as springboards to discussions that fit your style more appropriately. However, if an exercise seems a bit challenging, don't give up on it. As the saying goes, anything worth having is worth working for. In any case, the goal of this workbook is not simply to fortify your reading of *Saving Your Marriage Before It Starts*—the goal is to apply it, to make it real.

Exercises

24 SELF-TESTS
TO PUT THE BOOK
INTO ACTION

Exercise One

Your Personal Ten Commandments

This exercise is designed to help you uncover some of your unspoken rules. It will take about fifteen to twenty minutes.

Try to articulate some of the unspoken rules you grew up with. Take your time to think it over. These unspoken rules are generally so ingrained that we are rarely aware of them. If you're not married yet, by the way, you may have discovered some of your "rules" with a previous roommate.

We've provided you with sections to stimulate your thinking. The best way to come up with your own commandments is to think of what "unspoken rules" you grew up with in your family.

Rules about Finances

Example: "Credit cards are to be used only in an emergency."

1. _____

_____

2. _____

_____

Rules about Mealtime

Example: "Dinner should be served at the same time every night."

3. _____

_____

_____

4. _____

_____

_____

Rules about Chores

Example: "The towels from the laundry should be folded in thirds (not in half)."

5. _____

_____

_____

6. _____

_____

_____

Rules about Other Traditions and Holidays

Example: "You should open presents on Christmas Eve (not Christmas morning)."

7. _____

_____

_____

8. _____

_____

_____

Rules about Quirky Things

Example: "Never put a bottle of ketchup on the table (put it in a dish)."

9. _____

_____

_____

10. _____

_____

_____

Once both of you have written your "personal ten commandments," share them with each other.

As a man, think about how your dad modeled certain behaviors in each of these areas and consider how this may shape your expectations as a husband.

What surprises you about your partner's rules and why? Do some of her rules cause you to immediately push back?

Are there any specific rules you would like to change (on your side or hers)?

The more you talk about your unspoken rules, the less likely they are to affect your marriage in a negative way.

In addition, here's a helpful tip. Any time you have a fight or disagreement, ask yourself, "Is this fight a result of one of us breaking an unspoken rule?" If so, add that rule to your list and discuss how you will handle that situation in the future.

Making Your Roles Conscious

Listed below are a number of chores or life tasks that will need to be handled by you or your fiancée (wife). To make your unconscious understanding of roles conscious, first indicate how your parents handled these tasks. Then write down how you would like to divide up the tasks, according to your understanding of your own and your partner's interests, time, and abilities. Finally, compare your list with your partner's list, and discuss the results. Put your joint decision of who will do what in the last column, and be prepared to renegotiate when your circumstances change. This exercise will take about twenty to thirty minutes.

	Your Mother	Your Father	Both Parents	You	Your Spouse	Both of You	Final Decision
Providing income	☐	☐	☐	☐	☐	☐	_____
Staying home with children	☐	☐	☐	☐	☐	☐	_____
Paying bills and handling finances	☐	☐	☐	☐	☐	☐	_____
Yard work	☐	☐	☐	☐	☐	☐	_____
Gassing up the car	☐	☐	☐	☐	☐	☐	_____
Automobile maintenance	☐	☐	☐	☐	☐	☐	_____
Fixing things around the house	☐	☐	☐	☐	☐	☐	_____
Laundry	☐	☐	☐	☐	☐	☐	_____
Making the bed	☐	☐	☐	☐	☐	☐	_____
Doing the dishes	☐	☐	☐	☐	☐	☐	_____
Cleaning	☐	☐	☐	☐	☐	☐	_____
Cooking and baking	☐	☐	☐	☐	☐	☐	_____
Taking out the trash	☐	☐	☐	☐	☐	☐	_____
Grocery shopping	☐	☐	☐	☐	☐	☐	_____
Caring for a pet	☐	☐	☐	☐	☐	☐	_____
Scheduling social events	☐	☐	☐	☐	☐	☐	_____

	Your Mother	Your Father	Both Parents	You	Your Spouse	Both of You	Final Decision
Maintaining ties with friends and relatives	☐	☐	☐	☐	☐	☐	_____
Planning vacations	☐	☐	☐	☐	☐	☐	_____
Talking about spiritual matters	☐	☐	☐	☐	☐	☐	_____
Initiating sex	☐	☐	☐	☐	☐	☐	_____
Decorating the house	☐	☐	☐	☐	☐	☐	_____
Making major decisions	☐	☐	☐	☐	☐	☐	_____
Initiating discussion about the relationship	☐	☐	☐	☐	☐	☐	_____
Keeping the house neat and orderly	☐	☐	☐	☐	☐	☐	_____
Disciplining the children	☐	☐	☐	☐	☐	☐	_____
Shopping for other needs	☐	☐	☐	☐	☐	☐	_____
Other _____	☐	☐	☐	☐	☐	☐	_____
Other _____	☐	☐	☐	☐	☐	☐	_____

Once you have both filled out this list, compare notes and answer these three questions together:

1. What role behaviors do you tend to agree upon?
2. What role behaviors do you tend to see quite differently?
3. How are you going to adjust your expectations on the role behaviors where you are currently not in sync?

> We believe that some of these tasks (such as disciplining children or initiating sex) must be shared in order for the couple to have a strong relationship, but in reality many of the tasks may fall disproportionately to the husband or the wife because of unspoken assumptions or circumstances. Use this list periodically to discuss how you are doing, and readjust your roles or assignments if you need to.

Exercise Three

From Idealizing to Realizing
Your Partner

This exercise is designed to help you relinquish unrealistic ideals you
might hold about your partner and to discover her true character. It
will take about twenty to thirty minutes.

Begin by ranking on a one-to-seven scale how much the following
traits describe you and your partner. Complete the first two columns
("Your Ranking of You" and then "Your Ranking of Your Wife"). Don't
worry about the other two columns just yet.

Your Ranking of You		Your Ranking of Your Wife		Your Wife's Actual Rank		The Difference
___	Compassionate	___	-	___	=	___
___	Patient	___	-	___	=	___
___	Secure	___	-	___	=	___
___	Nurturing	___	-	___	=	___
___	Insightful	___	-	___	=	___
___	Confident	___	-	___	=	___
___	Relaxed	___	-	___	=	___
___	Tender	___	-	___	=	___
___	Even tempered	___	-	___	=	___
___	Honest	___	-	___	=	___
___	Healthy	___	-	___	=	___
___	Spiritual	___	-	___	=	___
___	Consistent	___	-	___	=	___

Once you have ranked the first two columns, share your rankings
with each other and write them on your own page. Then subtract your
partner's actual ranking of herself from your ranking of her. Note any
significant differences and discuss them.

Our three biggest differences in this exercise are:

1. _____

_____

2. _____

_____

3. _____

_____

One of the central tasks of the early marriage years is to move from "idealizing" your wife to "realizing" your wife. How accurate is your image of who your wife is compared to who she really is? The more accurately you can present yourselves to each other, the easier your first years of marriage will be.

Exercise Four

Exploring Unfinished Business

Marriage is not a quick fix for avoiding your own personal problems. In fact, marriage may even intensify those problems. This exercise is designed to help you honestly face the psychological and spiritual work you need to do as a person so that you do not look to your wife to fulfill needs that she cannot. It will take about twenty to thirty minutes.

Everyone has yearnings that were seldom, if ever, fulfilled in their relationship with their parents. Take a moment to reflect, and then write down some of the needs and desires you felt that were never really fulfilled by your parents. We've provided you with a few headings to stimulate your thinking, but don't let that limit you to just these categories.

Unfulfilled Needs for Encouragement

Example: "My parents never really encouraged my dreams or goals."

_____

_____

_____

Unfulfilled Needs for Praise

Example: "My parents never really celebrated my successes."

_____

_____

_____

Unfulfilled Needs for Listening

Example: "My parents never really understood me for who I am."

_____

_____

_____

_____

Unfulfilled Needs for Fun

Example: "My parents often thought I wasn't serious enough and wanted me to be more 'goal oriented.'"

_____

_____

_____

_____

Other Unfulfilled Needs That Shape My Expectations

Example: "I've never had anyone in my life who appreciates my creativity."

_____

_____

_____

_____

When we marry, we long to recreate the love and closeness and nurturance that we experienced or wished we had experienced in our relationship with our parents. But marriage is not always the place for those yearnings to be fulfilled. No human can meet another person's every need; deep relational longings are ultimately met only in a relationship with God.

If you are willing, share your writing with your partner and discuss the baggage you are both bringing into your marriage—and how your expectations of her as your wife might be shaped by your "unfinished business."

Exercise Five
Assessing Your Self-Image

This exercise is designed to help you measure your self-image and construct an interdependent relationship with your wife. It will take about twenty to thirty minutes.

"You cannot love another person unless you love yourself." Most of us have heard that statement so often we tend to dismiss it as just another catchphrase in the lexicon of pop psychology. But a solid sense of self-esteem is a vital element in building the capacity to love.

The following self-test can give you a quick evaluation of your self-esteem. Answer each with "yes," "usually," "seldom," or "no."

1. Do you believe strongly in certain values and principles, enough that you are willing to defend them?

Yes	Usually	Seldom	No

2. Do you act on your own best judgment, without regretting your actions if others disapprove?

Yes	Usually	Seldom	No

3. Do you avoid worrying about what is coming tomorrow or fussing over yesterday's or today's mistakes?

Yes	Usually	Seldom	No

4. Do you have confidence in your general ability to deal with problems, even in the face of failures and setbacks?

Yes	Usually	Seldom	No

5. Do you feel generally equal—neither inferior nor superior—to others?

Yes	Usually	Seldom	No

6. Do you take it more or less for granted that other people are interested in you and value you?

Yes	Usually	Seldom	No

7. Do you accept praise without pretense or false modesty, and accept compliments without feeling guilty?

Yes	Usually	Seldom	No

8. Do you resist the efforts of others to dominate you, especially your peers?

Yes	Usually	Seldom	No

9. Do you accept the idea—and admit to others—that you are capable of feeling a wide range of impulses and desires, ranging from anger to love, sadness to happiness, resentment to acceptance? (It does not follow, however, that you will act on all these feelings and desires.)

Yes	Usually	Seldom	No

10. Do you genuinely enjoy yourself in a wide range of activities, including work, play, creative self-expression, companionship, and just plain loafing?

Yes	Usually	Seldom	No

11. Do you sense and consider the needs of others?

Yes	Usually	Seldom	No

If your answer to most of the questions is "yes" or "usually," it's an indication that you have a sturdy sense of self-esteem. If most of your answers are "no" or "seldom," you may likely suffer from a low self-image and will need to strengthen it to build the best marriage. Research indicates that self-esteem has a lot to do with the way you will respond to your wife. People with a healthy self-image are more apt to express their opinions, are less sensitive to criticism, and are generally less preoccupied with themselves.

The point of this little self-test is not to accurately pinpoint your self-esteem. It's to generate a helpful discussion between the two of you. So, if you are willing, discuss your answers with each other and talk about how in reality you cannot make each other whole (though you can certainly help each other on the pathway to wholeness).

Exercise Six

Defining Love

This exercise will help you define love in your own terms and compare your definition with your partner's. It will take ten to fifteen minutes.

Researcher Beverly Fehr asked more than 170 people to rate the central features of love. The twelve most important attributes they identified are listed below. Take a moment to prioritize this list for yourself by placing a checkmark next to the top three qualities that are most important to you.

    ___ acceptance
    ___ caring
    ___ commitment
    ___ concern for the other's well-being
    ___ friendship
    ___ honesty
    ___ interest in the other
    ___ loyalty
    ___ respect
    ___ supportiveness
    ___ trust
    ___ wanting to be with the other

Next, write a brief definition of love that incorporates these qualities.

Love is ...

_____

_____

_____

Now, compare your priorities and your definition with your partner's to see what differences, if any, you might have when it comes to defining love.

Finally, complete these sentences to get a better feel for the application of your definition of love:

I feel most loved when you . . .

_____

_____

Though you may or may not know it, I'm showing you my love when I . . .

_____

_____

Exercise Seven

Getting Your Sex Life Off to a Great Start

This exercise is designed to help you dispel some common myths about sex and become more knowledgeable about lovemaking as a married couple.*

Below is a true and false questionnaire for you to complete. Don't worry about getting the right answers. Simply answer each item the best you can.

T   F   The key to sexual fulfillment is simply to do what comes naturally. In other words, let your instincts be your guide.

T   F   Most normal married couples have sexual intercourse about two to three times a week.

T   F   Because men typically have a stronger sex drive than women, it is primarily the husband's job to initiate sex—not the wife's.

T   F   When it comes down to it, men are almost always ready and willing to have sex, and a good wife should always be available for it.

T   F   The best way for a woman to have an orgasm is during intercourse.

T   F   While men have just one orgasm during sex, a woman must have multiple orgasms to be fulfilled sexually.

T   F   A man's erection is a signal that he is going to need intercourse or ejaculation.

T   F   The normal position for sexual intercourse is with the man on top.

T   F   To reach ultimate sexual fulfillment, a couple should strive for simultaneous orgasms, where both the husband and wife climax at the same time.

T   F   In general, the larger the man's penis, the more pleasurable sex is for the woman.

Number of True answers: _____   Number of False answers: _____

Once you have totaled your answers, compare notes and go through the following correct answers together. What matters here is not whether you answered correctly—the point is to learn more accurate information about your sex life as a married couple.

*We are indebted to Cliff and Joyce Penner and Louis and Melissa McBurney for the wealth of knowledge they provide in this area.

> T   F   The key to sexual fulfillment is simply to do what comes naturally.
>   In other words, let your instincts be your guide.

While many believe that if you are really good at sex you don't have to learn about it, the truth is that good sex requires much more than just doing what comes naturally. Therefore, one of the best ways to improve your sex life after marriage and to really enjoy it is to educate yourselves, experiment with each other, and teach each other. For example, this may mean reading a book from time to time about sexual intimacy in marriage. The more you learn about sex as a couple, especially each other's preferences and desires, the better your sex life will be. So the answer to this item is false.

> T   F   Most normal married couples have sexual intercourse about two
>   to three times a week.

When it comes to the frequency of sexual intercourse in your marriage, the two of you determine what is normal. You may have sex twice a day or twice per month. What matters is that, over the course of your married life, you talk about the best balance of your two sexual desires. So the answer to this item is false.

> T   F   Because men typically have a stronger sex drive than women,
>   it is primarily the husband's job to initiate sex—not the wife's.

Women have sexual urges and thoughts just as men do. In fact, women tend to fantasize even more than men. When women learn to express their sexual urges directly and share their creative fantasies, their husbands are delighted and their sex life is sparked. So it's not up to the man to always initiate sex, and the answer to this item is false. By the way, since women can be more particular about where, when, and how they want to be touched, it takes pressure off the husband and produces greater pleasure for the wife if she also takes the lead.

> T   F   When it comes down to it, men are almost always ready and
>   willing to have sex, and a good wife should always be available
>   for it.

Yikes! This false belief has led too many couples into trouble because it produces such incredible demand—on both partners. First, it demands that the husband behave as though he is interested even when he is not. And it also demands that the wife be responsive to her husband's arousal even when she is not interested. Truth be told, either one of you can decide to participate in a sexual time together when one of you is feeling the desire and the other is not, but it should not be by demand. Sex should always be a choice. As the Penners say, "Demand is a killer to a healthy, long-term sexual relationship."

> T   F   The best way for a woman to have an orgasm is during intercourse.

Here's the truth: The majority of women do not have orgasms during intercourse. While any woman can learn to be orgasmic during intercourse if she desires to, most women respond orgasmically to manual clitoral stimulation. Of course, some women only respond during intercourse and others respond either way. All variations are delightful ways of receiving sexual pleasure and release, but have nothing to do with "the right way." What is right is what works for you. And keep in mind that the stimulation that triggers the orgasm in the woman has nothing to do with the man or his masculinity. As you both listen to your inner desires and communicate those desires to each other and respond to each other's invitations, the automatic response orgasm is more likely to happen. So the answer to this item is false.

> T   F   While men have just one orgasm during sex, a woman must have multiple orgasms to be fulfilled sexually.

The number of orgasms a woman experiences during sex is not an indicator of her level of sexual fulfillment. Many women are totally satisfied after one release. Others quickly get restimulated and desire more. So, for the man, there's no need to equate the number of orgasms with his level of "performance." So the answer to this item is false.

> T   F   A man's erection is a signal that he is going to need intercourse or ejaculation.

An erection simply means a man is aroused, and that's all. An erection for the man is no different than vaginal lubrication for the woman. It's not a demand for action, even though many men say they just cannot handle getting aroused and not having an ejaculation. The truth is that all men get erections every eighty to ninety minutes while they sleep, but these erections rarely lead to an ejaculation. It is equally possible to allow arousal to come and go during caressing or in response to seeing his wife's body. So, again, the answer to this item is false.

> T   F   The normal position for sexual intercourse is with the man on top.

The man-on-top position is commonly used by many couples, but that does not make it the normal or right position. With more sexual experiences together in your marriage, you will discover positions that bring you the most pleasure. You need to feel free to try a variety of positions in your lovemaking. So the answer is false.

> T   F   To reach ultimate sexual fulfillment, a couple should strive for simultaneous orgasms, where both the husband and wife climax at the same time.

Having simultaneous orgasms can be fun if it happens, but it's an unnecessary goal to put on your lovemaking. It has absolutely nothing to do with how successful you are as a couple. The demand for both spouses to have orgasms at the same time gets in the way of the pleasure of enjoying each other. Many couples prefer separate orgasms so each one can experience the other's. So, again, the answer is false.

> T   F   In general, the larger the man's penis, the more pleasurable sex is for the woman.

Penis size is the source of many myths. But in truth, it has nothing to do with a man's sexuality, his attractiveness to his wife, his skill as a lover, or the satisfaction he can bring to his wife. The quality of sex is not in any way related to penis size. When erect, penises vary little in size from one to another. A smaller, flaccid penis enlarges proportionately more when erect than does a larger flaccid penis. Also, the vagina adapts to the penis, and it is only in the outer third of the vagina that the woman reasons to the penis. The shortest penis is more than adequate to bring pleasure to a woman. So the answer is false. The penis myths perpetuated by locker-room jokes have nothing to do with reality.

So, each of the ten items in this self-test is false. If you answered any of them as true, don't feel badly. Each of these items represents one of the most common myths about marital sex. And now that you know the truth, you are far more likely to get your sex life off to a great start.

Of course, to augment your sexual knowledge, you will also need a solid understanding of the male and female anatomy. You have probably already studied this in school, but even so, it's very helpful to brush up on this information. Cliff and Joyce Penner's bestselling book *The Gift of Sex* is a terrific resource for this, as is Louis and Melissa McBurney's book *Real Questions, Real Answers About Sex*.

We want to leave you with one more thought. Remember that one of the keys to a great sex life is to talk openly about it as husband and wife. Far too many married couples simply don't discuss their sex life together. Once you are married, we recommend that you talk in specific terms by completing such sentences as:

I feel sexually aroused by you when …
When we are making love, I really enjoy …
When we are making love, I feel uncomfortable when you …
The surest turnoff for me is …
The surest turn-on for me is …
What you need to know about me when it comes to sex is …

These kinds of specific statements will do wonders for your sex life right from the start and ensure "hot monogamy" for decades.

Exercise Eight

Your Changing Love Style

This exercise will help you understand how love is not stagnant and how the love you have for each other will change during different life passages. It will take twenty-five to thirty minutes.

Using the triangular model of love described in chapter 2 (passion, intimacy, and commitment), draw how your love style with your partner has changed over time. You may want to divide your relationship into three phases and then draw the love triangle that best suits each phase. In other words, if early on passion was stronger than commitment and intimacy, draw a triangle (identifying each side) representing that, and so on.

First third of our relationship

Second third of our relationship

Third third of our relationship

As we grow and develop, each stage of the life cycle is marked by the emergence of a new form of love. This means that during certain phases of life, some sides of the triangle will get more attention than others. Using the triangular model of love, draw how your love might look in future passages of marriage (e.g., how will it look in five years or even fifty years).

Discuss with your partner how you feel about the inevitability of love taking on different forms in your future.

Exercise Nine
Cultivating Intimacy

This exercise will help you open your heart and increase your level of intimacy.

Begin by writing about your shared experiences. What is it about your backgrounds that draws you together? What things set the two of you apart from others? What experiences have you had together that bring back fond memories?

_____

_____

_____

_____

Next, focus on things that the two of you share. Begin by jotting down one or two things in each of the following categories, then discuss them with your partner. The more detailed you can be, the better.

• Interests we have in common include:

_____

_____

_____

• Plans we share for our future include:

_____

_____

_____

_____

• Fears and anxieties we both have include:

_____

_____

_____

• Hopes and dreams we share include:

_____

_____

_____

• Spiritual beliefs we both have include:

_____

_____

_____

Conclude this exercise by talking in specific terms about what the two of you can do to cultivate more emotional intimacy in your relationship.

Listening to Your Self-Talk

This exercise will help you and your partner examine how much your attitude shapes the moods of your marriage. It will take about ten to fifteen minutes.

List three circumstances that typically get you into a rotten mood. For example: being stuck in traffic, waiting for someone who is late to arrive, having your credit card rejected, and so on.

1. _____

   _____

2. _____

   _____

3. _____

   _____

There is a maxim in psychology that says "you feel what you think." In other words, your feelings are the result of what is going on in your mind. For each of the bad circumstances you listed above, write down what you are saying to yourself that makes you feel so rotten. For example: "I could be playing tennis instead of being stuck on this freeway."

1. _____

   _____

2. _____

   _____

3. _____

   _____

Now, exercise your power to choose your own attitude by changing your self-talk. Write three alternative statements that would not lead to feeling so rotten. For example: "At least I can use this time to just relax and mentally rehearse my tennis serve."

1. _____

_____

2. _____

_____

3. _____

_____

Negative self-talk can also affect our responses to more serious situations. To see how negative self-talk may have affected you, list two situations in your life that were difficult or painful to deal with. For example: losing a job, breaking off a relationship, or going through a serious illness.

1. _____

_____

2. _____

_____

For each of the crises you listed above, write down things you said to yourself that added to your pain. For example: "I was fired from my job because I'm a natural-born loser."

1. _____

_____

_____

2. _____

_____

_____

Again, exercise your power to choose your own attitude by changing your self-talk. Write two alternative statements that did help or could have helped you adapt to the situation and grow through it. For example: "I will learn from my mistakes and, with God's help, make sure they don't happen again."

1. _____

_____

_____

2. _____

_____

_____

Talk about this exercise with your partner. Discuss how changing your self-talk can improve your chances for marital happiness. How can the two of you team up to fight negative self-talk?

Exercise Eleven
Avoiding the Blame Game

This exercise will help you and your partner take responsibility for your own attitudes. It will take about ten to fifteen minutes.

Below are several scenarios where blame typically enters the picture. For each scenario, decide on your own who is to blame.

First Scene

It's Valentine's Day. Mary has prepared a special meal for Dan—all his favorite foods. She also made him a special valentine. Dan, however, didn't get Mary anything. After dinner, Dan thanks Mary for the food and slumps into a chair in front of the television. Mary, feeling hurt, leaves the dirty dishes in the sink and goes into the bedroom to cry. Dan realizes what just happened, follows her into the bedroom, and the two accuse each other of being insensitive. Who is at fault?

Dan is to blame   Mary is to blame

Second Scene

Aaron and Kim are having dinner with another couple. During the casual conversation, Kim jokingly makes fun of Aaron's shirt. He laughs at first but soon he becomes withdrawn, and the conversation becomes noticeably strained. When they get home, both of them accuse the other of ruining the evening. Who is at fault?

Aaron is to blame   Kim is to blame

Third Scene

On a whim, Carl buys a new CD player on sale. He and Michelle had talked about getting one, but they'd decided to wait another year. Carl, however, felt the bargain was too good to pass up and also thought it would be a nice surprise for Michelle. It wasn't. All Michelle could think about was how they were saving money for plane tickets to see her family at Christmas. Carl and Michelle blamed each other for being too controlling with their money. Who is at fault?

Carl is to blame   Michelle is to blame

You may now compare your answers with each other, but there are no "correct" responses. It doesn't matter who is to blame. It doesn't matter who is at fault. What matters in building a happy marriage is defining what the problem is and seeing how each of you can be a part of the solution. Take time to read through the scenarios again, placing yourselves in the couple's shoes. What could each of you do to avoid playing the blame game in these instances?

Adjusting to Things Beyond Your Control

This exercise will help you and your partner more effectively adjust to the jolts of life. It will take about ten to fifteen minutes.

The book talked about how different the Christmas story would be if Mary and Joseph had not had the capacity to adjust to circumstances beyond their control. What situations or circumstances in your relationship (including your wedding if you are already married) have already thrown you for a loop? Jot down two or three particular challenges you did not anticipate:

_____

_____

_____

_____

_____

How did you respond to these unexpected situations? List some things you did to keep your chin up and some things you did that didn't work as well.

Positive Ways I Coped	Negative Ways I Coped

Now compare your coping strategies with your partner's. In what ways can the two of you improve your capacities to adjust? How can you be better equipped to maintain a positive outlook when similar unexpected circumstances arise in the future?

Conclude this exercise by discussing what will happen in your marriage if you do not practice your ability to adjust to things beyond your control.

Exercise Thirteen
How Well Do You Communicate?

This self-test is designed to help you assess how well you communicate with your partner. It will take about ten minutes. Answer the questions as honestly as you can. The more honest you are, the more meaningful the exercise will be.

1. When your partner is in a bad mood, you are likely to:
   A. Ask whether she's getting her period.
   B. Leave her alone until she's feeling better.
   C. Ask her what's wrong.

2. She says you don't tell her often enough that you love her. You reply:
   A. "I tell you I love you all the time."
   B. "You know I love you. Why do I have to say it?"
   C. "I love you very much. Sometimes I just forget to say so."

3. You are watching television, and she says she'd like to talk to you. You say:
   A. "How about ten o'clock?"
   B. "Anytime you want."
   C. "Sorry, I'm in the middle of something right now."

4. How often do you win arguments with your partner?
   A. Almost always
   B. Almost never
   C. I try not to think in terms of winning or losing.

5. Your partner wants to talk about some difficulties she is having at work. Would you most likely:

    A. Point out that you have work problems of your own?

    B. Offer helpful advice?

    C. Listen and try to be supportive?

6. For the second time this week you find that she didn't run an errand as she had promised. Annoyed, you:

    A. Tell her how much it irritates you and do it yourself.

    B. Pout a bit and ask her to do it tomorrow.

    C. "Forget" to do something for her next time she asks.

7. You're in a romantic mood, but when you reach for her she just yawns. You:

    A. Feel rejected and say, "Whew, it's cold in here."

    B. Ask her why she isn't responding.

    C. Let her know your desires but adjust if she is not in sync.

Scoring: For questions one, two, four, five, and seven, give yourself one point for each "A" answer, two for each "B," and three for each "C." Then on questions three and six, give yourself three points for each "A," two for each "B," and one for each "C."

7 to 11 points: Hiding your feelings is one of the fastest ways you can ruin a relationship. You need to learn how to listen to your partner and how to talk with her. Chapter 6 will show you how.

12 to 17 points: You're doing well, but you need to remember that your partner needs your support and encouragement much more than she needs your advice. You can really benefit from practicing some of the skills discussed in chapter 6.

18 to 21 points: You're doing quite well in the area of communication, but there's always room for improvement. Chapter 6 will help you fine-tune some skills you are already good at.

Exercise Fourteen

The Daily Temperature Reading

This exercise will help you and your partner maintain an easy flow of communication about the big and little things going on in your lives. It will take about thirty minutes.

At first this exercise may seem artificial and even hokey. But in time you'll evolve your own style and find that it is invaluable for staying close. Do it daily, perhaps during a meal. Here are the basics. Sit close, holding each other's hands (touch creates an atmosphere of acceptance), then follow these five steps:

1. *Appreciation.* Take turns expressing appreciation for something your partner has done. Thank each other.
2. *New Information.* In the absence of information, assumptions (often false ones) rush in. Tell your partner something new ("We finally got a new account executive at work"). Let your partner in on your life, and then listen to the news your partner shares.
3. *Puzzles.* Take turns asking each other something you don't understand but your partner can explain: "Why were you so down last night?" Or voice a concern about yourself: "I don't know why I got so angry while I was balancing the checkbook yesterday."
4. *Complaint with Request.* Without being judgmental, cite a specific behavior that bothers you and state the behavior you are asking for instead. "When you clean the top of the stove, please dry it with a paper towel. If you don't, it leaves streaks."
5. *Hopes.* Share your hopes, from the mundane ("I hope we have sunshine this weekend") to the grandiose ("I'd really love to spend a month in Europe with you").

These simple steps have worked for many couples who want to keep the channels of communication open.

Exercise Fifteen
I Can Hear Clearly Now

Your partner will often hide important feelings behind her words. Reflecting her feelings is one of the most helpful and difficult listening techniques to implement. Following are some statements that a wife might make. Read each separately, listening for feelings. Make note of the feeling you hear, and write out a response which reflects that feeling for each of the statements.

1. "I don't want your advice!"

_____

_____

2. "Karen doesn't seem to call me like she used to."

_____

_____

3. "I am so tired of never knowing when you are going to get home."

_____

_____

4. "I'd like to ask for a raise, but what if I don't get it?"

_____

_____

5. "Just once I'd like not to have to pick your coat off this chair."

_____

_____

_____

Now compare your list of reflective statements to those listed below to see how accurately you recognized feelings. Give yourself a 2 on those items where your choice closely matches, a 1 on items where your choice only partially matches, and a 0 if you missed altogether.

Possible Responses to the Exercise in Active Listening:

1. "Sounds like you'd just like to be understood."
2. "You must feel kind of hurt."
3. "You sound so frustrated; let's work this thing out."
4. "Sounds like you are feeling anxious and a little afraid."
5. "That's got to be aggravating. I'll make it a point not to do that so much."

How You Rate on Recognizing Feelings:

8–10   Above average recognition of feelings

5–7   Average recognition of feelings

0–4   Below average recognition of feelings

Exercise Sixteen
Couple's Inventory

This exercise will help you take stock of the roles you both play, consciously and unconsciously, in your relationship. It will take about twenty to thirty minutes.

Complete the following sentences as honestly as you can.

1. I am important to our marriage because _____

_____

2. What I contribute to my partner's success is _____

_____

3. I feel central to our relationship when _____

_____

4. I feel peripheral to our relationship when _____

_____

5. The ways I have fun with you are _____

_____

6. The way I get space for myself in our relationship is _____

_____

7. The ways I am intimate with you are _____

_____

8. The role I play as your husband is _____

_____

9. I feel most masculine in our relationship when _____

_____

10. I deal with stress by _____

_____

11. The division of labor in household tasks is decided by _____

_____

12. Our finances are controlled by _____

_____

13. How we spend our spare time is determined by _____

_____

14. Our social life is planned by _____

_____

15. I need you to _____

_____

Compare your statements with each other and discuss how being a man influences the way you responded.

Exercise Seventeen

Your Top Ten Needs

This exercise will help you identify some of your deepest needs in a marriage relationship and communicate those needs to your partner. It will take about twenty to thirty minutes.

Listed below are some of the most common needs that people identify as being important in marriage. Rate how important each of these items is for you. If you wish to add other items not included in our list, please do so. As always, do this on your own before discussing it with your partner.

	Not that important						Very important
Admiration	1	2	3	4	5	6	7
Affection	1	2	3	4	5	6	7
Commitment	1	2	3	4	5	6	7
Companionship	1	2	3	4	5	6	7
Conversation	1	2	3	4	5	6	7
Financial support	1	2	3	4	5	6	7
Honesty	1	2	3	4	5	6	7
Intimacy	1	2	3	4	5	6	7
Personal space	1	2	3	4	5	6	7
Respect	1	2	3	4	5	6	7
Rootedness	1	2	3	4	5	6	7
Security	1	2	3	4	5	6	7
Sex	1	2	3	4	5	6	7
Shared activities	1	2	3	4	5	6	7
_____	1	2	3	4	5	6	7
_____	1	2	3	4	5	6	7

Now that you have completed your list, rank them in order of importance. Next, share the results with your partner.

What needs do both of you identify as important?

Discuss what needs are most important to you personally. As you discuss them, explain what that need means to you. Men and women often mean different things even when they use the same word (e.g., intimacy).

Finally, discuss how each of your needs might change as you grow in marriage.

Exercise Eighteen

Identifying Your Hot Topics

This exercise will help you put your finger on those issues that are especially prone to cause conflict in your relationship. It will take about twenty minutes.

Listed below are the common relationship issues that most couples will encounter from time to time over the course of the relationship. Rate how much of a problem each issue is for you right now. If you wish to add other areas not included in our list, please do so. As always, do this on your own before discussing it with your partner.

	Not at all a problem						Very much a problem
Careers	1	2	3	4	5	6	7
Children	1	2	3	4	5	6	7
Chores	1	2	3	4	5	6	7
Communication	1	2	3	4	5	6	7
Friends	1	2	3	4	5	6	7
Illness	1	2	3	4	5	6	7
In-laws	1	2	3	4	5	6	7
Jealousy	1	2	3	4	5	6	7
Money	1	2	3	4	5	6	7
Priorities	1	2	3	4	5	6	7
Recreation	1	2	3	4	5	6	7
Relatives	1	2	3	4	5	6	7
Religion	1	2	3	4	5	6	7
Sex	1	2	3	4	5	6	7
Sleep habits	1	2	3	4	5	6	7
_____	1	2	3	4	5	6	7
_____	1	2	3	4	5	6	7

Now that you have completed your list, share the results with your partner. What issues are "hot" for both of you, and what issues are "hot" for one or the other of you? Next, discuss what issues might become more troublesome in the future and what you can do to calm the conflict before it erupts.

Exercise Nineteen

Money Talks and So Can We

This exercise will help you delve into money matters that will impact your marriage in countless ways. It may take a bit longer than some of the other exercises in this workbook, but it is immensely practical and will benefit you for decades.

Your Family and Money

You already know from earlier exercises that your family of origin shapes nearly everything you do. And how you relate to money is not an exception. So let's begin by having you simply note how money was treated, valued, and managed in your home growing up. How did your childhood shape your beliefs about money? Make a few notes here so that you can discuss it in a moment with your partner. Be sure to note how you think you are similar or different than your parents when it comes to money matters. And also note how you see money being managed in your home together.

_____

_____

_____

_____

The Money Self-Test

What follows is a series of statements for you to rate. There are no right or wrong answers, and don't try to answer how you think others might want you to. Be honest. This is a self-test that will help you and your partner get real about personal finances.

1. I feel comfortable talking about finances with my partner.

   Never   Rarely   Sometimes   Often   Always

2. I pay bills on time.

   Never   Rarely   Sometimes   Often   Always

3. I pay off my credit card balance every month.

Never	Rarely	Sometimes	Often	Always

4. I save a portion of my income every month.

Never	Rarely	Sometimes	Often	Always

5. I give a predetermined portion of my money to charities or my church every month.

Never	Rarely	Sometimes	Often	Always

6. I manage my money with a set budget that I follow.

Never	Rarely	Sometimes	Often	Always

7. I buy things on impulse.

Never	Rarely	Sometimes	Often	Always

8. Most people who know me well would say I'm a saver and rather tight with my money.

Never	Rarely	Sometimes	Often	Always

9. I know how much I have in my bank account at almost any given time.

Never	Rarely	Sometimes	Often	Always

10. I regularly keep track of what I spend and where I spend it.

Never	Rarely	Sometimes	Often	Always

11. When it comes to investing, I give serious thought to and study how I can invest my money for high returns in the long run.

Never	Rarely	Sometimes	Often	Always

Once you have completed this self-test, take a few minutes to talk with your partner about money matters. Begin by discussing how your families approached finances. And keep in mind that this discussion is simply about getting money matters on the table. It's not about judging each other's approaches. And as you compare your answers on your two self-tests, note each item where your answers are quite divergent.

Here are a few questions to help you organize your findings:

1. Do you have the same or different views on spending styles, credit, and debt?

_____

_____

2. Your views on giving and saving money and investing for the future?

_____

_____

3. Your views on working with a financial plan and budget?

_____

_____

Do You Clash over Cash?

After this discussion, rank on the following continuum where the two of you might fall when it comes to money matters:

Out of sync   In sync

1	2	3	4	5	6	7	8	9	10

Don't be disturbed if you find you have many divergent views on finances as a couple. Most couples do. What matters is what you are going to do about it. What follows are practical suggestions to help you begin implementing a proven plan.

If Either One of You Is in Debt, Start Digging Out

If you haven't done so already, each of you needs to be up front with the other about where you are personally on your finances as it relates to debt. We've seen many couples who get married only to discover that their partner has a significant amount of debt that was never disclosed beforehand. Don't allow this to happen to you, and don't hold back this kind of information from your partner. You will wrestle with trust issues for decades as a result of not being up front early on. And it's simple. It basically involves answering three primary questions:

50

1. Do you have credit card debt? If so, how much?
2. Do you have loans you are paying off? If so, how much?
3. Do you owe anyone money? If so, how much?

Now if either of you has financial debt, you need to devise a plan together for getting out of it as soon as possible. If the debt is significant, this may mean talking with a financial consultant who specializes in these matters. One of the most respected and successful do-it-yourself programs comes from Dave Ramsey, and you can visit his website at *www.daveramsey.com*. You'll want to implement a cash control system, for example, and you will find all the tools you need for this at his site. Digging out of debt is the first order of business in getting on your feet financially as a couple.

Design a Budget

Whether you have debt or not, we strongly recommend that you design a budget together as a couple. Why? Because a budget allows you to control your money rather than the other way around. And it's not as bad as you might imagine. It begins by getting an accurate picture of your total income and then deciding how you will allocate it. Of course, this may be revised as circumstances change, but you've got to start somewhere. Here's a budget worksheet that will help you get going:

Basic Budget Worksheet

CATEGORY	MONTHLY BUDGET AMOUNT	MONTHLY ACTUAL AMOUNT	DIFFERENCE BETWEEN ACTUAL AND BUDGET
INCOME:			
Wages Paid			
Bonuses			
Interest Income			
Capital Gains Income			
Dividend Income			
Miscellaneous Income			
INCOME SUBTOTAL			

CATEGORY	MONTHLY BUDGET AMOUNT	MONTHLY ACTUAL AMOUNT	DIFFERENCE BETWEEN ACTUAL AND BUDGET
EXPENSES:			
Mortgage or Rent			
TV Cable			
Telephone			
Home Repairs/ Maintenance			
Car Payments			
Gasoline/Oil			
Auto Repairs/ Maintenance/Fees			
Other Transportation (tolls, bus, subway, etc.)			
Child Care			
Auto Insurance			
Home Owner's/ Renter's Insurance			
Computer Expense			
Entertainment/ Recreation			
Groceries			
Toiletries, Household Products			
Clothing			
Eating Out			
Gifts/Donations/Tithe			
Health Care (medical/dental/vision, incl. insurance)			
Hobbies			
Interest Expense (mortgage, credit cards, fees)			
Magazines/Newspapers			
Federal Income Tax			

CATEGORY	MONTHLY BUDGET AMOUNT	MONTHLY ACTUAL AMOUNT	DIFFERENCE BETWEEN ACTUAL AND BUDGET
State Income Tax			
Social Security/ Medicare Tax			
Personal Property Tax			
Pets			
Miscellaneous Expenses			
EXPENSES SUBTOTAL			
NET INCOME (INCOME LESS EXPENSES)			

Here's How to Use This Worksheet:

- Go through your checkbook or bills for the last two to three months and add and delete categories from the worksheet to fit your expenditures.
- Think about your hobbies and your habits and be sure to add categories for these expenses.
- Go through your pay stubs and calculate your average monthly gross pay. Do the same for any interest income, dividends, bonuses, or other miscellaneous income.
- For each expense category, try to determine a budget amount that realistically reflects your actual expenses while setting targeted spending levels that will enable you to save money.
- If an expense is incurred more or less often than monthly, convert it to a monthly amount when calculating the monthly budget amount. For instance, an auto expense that is billed every six months would be converted to monthly by dividing the six-month premium by six.
- Once you're comfortable with your expense categories and budgeted amounts, enter expenditures from your checkbook from the last month.
- Keep track of cash expenditures throughout the month and total and categorize these at the end of each month.

- Subtotal the income and expense categories. Subtract the total expenses from the total income to arrive at your net income.
- If the number is negative, your expenses are greater than your income. Your situation can probably be greatly improved by changing your spending habits.
- After you've tracked your actual spending for a month or two, analyze your spending to identify where you can comfortably make cuts.
- Once you've got the budgeting process in place, take an in-depth look at your largest spending categories, brainstorm about ways to reduce spending in specific categories, and set realistic goals.

Keep this in mind: One of the top reasons, if not *the* top reason, so many people fail at budgeting is attitude. If you think of it as a penny-pinching sacrifice instead of a means for achieving your financial goals and dreams, how long are you likely to stick with it? Many people refuse to budget because of budgeting's negative connotation. If you're one of these people, try thinking of it as a "spending plan" instead of a "budget." It's like the difference between going on a diet and eating healthily. One is negative and restrictive; the other is positive and allows you to indulge now and then and still achieve your goals.

Talk about Your Financial Goals

Throughout your marriage you will talk about financial goals from time to time, but this is an important topic at the start as well. So take another moment or two to consider where you and your partner would like to be financially in another year, another five years, ten years, and so on. Here are some questions to generate this discussion:

1. What are your thoughts on owning your own home?
2. Have you considered how your finances will be impacted by having children?
3. Do you have a plan for paying off car loans?
4. What are your goals when it comes to giving money away and supporting causes you believe in?

Exercise Twenty

Mind Reading

This exercise will help you bring true and false assumptions you are making about your partner into the open so there are fewer surprises and conflicts. It will take about ten minutes.

Normally, trying to "mind read" what your partner is thinking is not a healthy habit (because it will lead you to jump to irrational conclusions). That's why in this exercise you will actually assess the accuracy of your assumptions before acting on them.

Here's how it works. The next time you sense that your partner is upset with you, pause for a moment and say, "I want to read your mind." Then tell her what you think she was saying to herself. For example, "I think you are mad about the way I left the bed this morning," or "I think you are upset because I wanted to watch TV instead of take a walk." Then say, "How accurate am I?" Your partner can then rate how accurate you are on a percentage scale. For example, she might say, "That's about 20 percent accurate," or "That's 100 percent accurate."

This simple exercise can be done anytime you sense that your partner is upset and you'd like to know if you are right about the reasons for it. Every couple mind reads every day. This exercise just makes that habit up front and more useful.

To get the feel of how this exercise works, consider how your partner was thinking or feeling about something in your relationship that happened within the last couple of days. Of course, this exercise is most helpful when used in the present tense (while you are in the midst of an experience), but to get the hang of it you'll bring up something that's already happened—something that you never really processed but made assumptions about (e.g., you think she was upset when you didn't show up on time). Once you have that in mind, complete this sentence:

I think you were . . .

Now, ask her how accurate you are in this assumption and note it on the following scale:

Completely Inaccurate   Right on the Money

    1   2   3   4   5   6   7   8   9   10

Again, the point of this simple exercise is to diffuse your natural inclination to "mind read" by making your assumptions known. You'll be amazed how handy this can be in the midst of an intense conversation.

Exercise Twenty-One
Sharing Withholds

This exercise will help you and your partner keep a clean emotional slate and avoid needless conflicts. We call it "sharing withholds" because it gives you the chance to share thoughts and feelings you may have withheld from each other. It will take about ten to fifteen minutes, and many couples find it helpful to do this exercise on a weekly basis.

Begin by writing two things your partner has done in the last forty-eight hours that you sincerely appreciated but did not tell her. For example, "I appreciate the compliment you gave me as I got out of the car yesterday, and I never did tell you," or "I appreciate the help you gave me in writing my proposal last night, and I don't think you know how much that meant to me."

I appreciate . . .

_____

I appreciate . . .

_____

Next, write one thing your partner has done in the last forty-eight hours that irritated you, but which you did not say anything about. For example, "I didn't like it when you borrowed my umbrella without telling me," or "I didn't like it when you said nothing about the meal I prepared for us last night."

I didn't like it when . . .

_____

Once both of you have written your statements, take turns sharing them. One person shares all three statements one after the other—we recommend sandwiching the negative withhold between the two positives when you share them. Then the other person shares his or her three statements. And here is an important part of this exercise. The person on the receiving end can say only "thank you" after each statement. That's all. Just "thank you." This rule allows couples to share something that bugs them without fearing a blowup or a defensive reaction. It also allows couples to receive critiques in the context of affirmation.

Here's another important piece to this exercise. Once you've both shared your withholds, neither of you can talk about the negative withhold you just heard for thirty minutes. Why? Because in a half hour's time you will have become more rational and thoughtful. At that point you can then ask your partner questions about it and are far less likely to have an emotional reaction. At that time, too, you may simply be inclined to offer an apology if appropriate. The point is not to stir up a fight where there was none. The point is to clear the "emotional land mines" from your marriage by keeping you current and not allowing painful wounds, even minor ones, to fester.

This exercise can be done weekly as we mentioned. Once you get the hang of it, you don't necessarily need to write your statements down, but it's often helpful. You may also want to agree on a routine time when you can do this exercise each week (e.g., Wednesdays after dinner) so one of you doesn't have to always initiate it. If you put this into practice by making it a weekly habit, we think you'll agree that sharing withholds can save you hundreds of hours of needless bickering.

Exercise Twenty-Two
Your Spiritual Journey

This exercise will help you and your partner share your individual pilgrimages. It will take about fifteen to twenty-five minutes.

Part of cultivating spiritual intimacy comes from merging two individual journeys. We are all beginners when it comes to spiritual development, but each of us has come from a different place and traveled a different road to meet where we are today. You may have grown up in a religious home learning Bible verses, going to Sunday school, and studying at a Christian college. Or maybe you never went to church while growing up and are just becoming grounded in your faith. Whatever your story, take a moment to gather your thoughts about your own spiritual quest. Then make a few notes of some of the significant mile markers.

Next, take a moment to complete this brief quiz.

Agree	Disagree	Spouses should . . .
☐	☐	Pray together every day.
☐	☐	Study the Bible together regularly.
☐	☐	Discuss spiritual issues.
☐	☐	Go to the same church.
☐	☐	Agree on theology.
☐	☐	Pay a tithe.
☐	☐	Pray for each other.
☐	☐	Leave each other's spiritual life up to God.
☐	☐	Have the same level of spiritual maturity.
☐	☐	Attend church at least once a week.

Once you have gathered your thoughts and completed the quiz, share your journey with your partner. Discuss what has brought you to where you are today. Also, compare how each of you responded to the quiz. Use it as a springboard to a deeper discussion of how each of you views spiritual matters.

Next, seek to understand how both you and your partner love God. This can be revolutionary for some couples. Gary Thomas, in his helpful book *Sacred Pathways*, describes nine ways we tend to relate to God.* Rank the top two or three styles that fit you best. Then try to predict your partner's top pathways before comparing notes.

Me	My Partner	
☐	☐	*The Traditionalist* loves God through rituals, sacraments, and symbols throughout the year.
☐	☐	*The Visionary* loves God by dreaming a great dream to accomplish great things.
☐	☐	*The Socialite* loves God best around other people, confiding in them and being accountable to them.
☐	☐	*The Intellectual* seeks God with his or her mind by considering a new theological concept.
☐	☐	*The Caregiver* loves God by being compassionate and loving others even if it means significant sacrifice.
☐	☐	*The Contemplative* seeks to love God in a quiet pursuit of journaling and reflection.
☐	☐	*The Activist* is at war with injustice and loves God by fighting it.
☐	☐	*The Naturalist* feels closest to God in the out-of-doors in the midst of creation.
☐	☐	*The Worshiper* is inspired by joyful celebration and music.

*Gary Thomas, *Sacred Pathways* (Grand Rapids, Mich.: Zondervan, 2002).

Now, jot down some specific ways these pathways are manifested in your life. If you are a Contemplative, for example, what do you like to do, where do you like to go, and how much time do you like to spend, to be close to God?

_____

_____

_____

Once you and your partner have both noted the top two or three styles that fit you best, spend a few minutes comparing them and discuss what you might learn from each other's pathways.

Improving Your Serve

This exercise will help you and your partner cultivate a soulful marriage by reaching out to others. It will take about ten to fifteen minutes.

Here are a few of the ways couples have practiced the fine art of serving others:

- Volunteering in a youth group
- Supporting someone's education
- Taking care of a shut-in's lawn
- Welcoming new people to the neighborhood
- Doing short-term relief trips overseas
- Sending helpful books to people

Take a moment and list a few ways that you and your partner might reach out together as a team. Work on your own and be as creative as you can before sharing your thoughts with your partner.

_____

_____

_____

_____

_____

_____

Now compare your list with your partner's. Combine your lists and begin to rank the items in order of what both of you might like to do as a team. Once you have a couple of things that seem like they might fit your joint style, discuss in more detail what they might actually look like.

1. How would the two of you actually live out these forms of service?

2. What do you think reaching out to others might do for your marriage?

Exercise Twenty-Four

Study Your Spouse

This exercise will help you understand your partner's unique needs now and in the future. It will take about five to ten minutes *each day.*

No one can play as significant a role in encouraging your partner as you. No one can meet her needs better than you. But to be effective, you must study your partner by paying careful attention to her needs, desires, and aspirations.

This exercise is simply a prayer. It need not involve any sharing or discussion with your partner. It simply asks you to study and pray.

> *God, our Creator, you were there when my partner was formed. You knit her together in her mother's womb. You know her every thought, need, and desire. You are acquainted with all her ways. Enlighten me. Teach me to know this complicated woman you have given me to love.*

Record any of your thoughts or observations below as you consider how you can better understand and study your soul mate. How does your new understanding of your partner change the way you treat her? Here are a few follow-up questions to help you structure your thoughts and review the content of *Saving Your Marriage Before It Starts*:

1. What can you keep in mind about her expectations (shaped by the family she came from) that will allow you to have a deeper understanding of her?

2. As you think about her definition of love (what makes her feel loved by you) as well as the three essential ingredients of love (passion, intimacy, and commitment), what are the actions you can intentionally take and observations you can make to express your love to her?

_____

_____

_____

_____

3. When you think about "the habit of happiness" as it relates to her, what can you keep in mind about her internal "self-talk" and what helps her to keep a positive attitude?

_____

_____

_____

_____

4. What kinds of conversations does she most enjoy, and when are you most likely to experience them?

_____

_____

_____

_____

5. As you bridge the gender gap in your marriage, what will serve you well to keep in mind about her as a woman?

_____

_____

_____

_____

6. What issues are most likely to result in frustration and tension for her (what are her hot topics?), and what can you learn to do better to resolve conflicts with her?

_____

_____

_____

_____

7. As you consider her spiritual journey, what can you do to help her carve out a path to God that is meaningful in your marriage?

_____

_____

_____

_____

Study your partner. Listen to her, talk to her. And every day, pray this simple prayer, asking God to help you understand her better.

Sessions

FOR GROUP OR COUPLE
DISCUSSION WITH
THE DVD CURRICULUM

Introduction

Studying this material in a group with other couples is one of the best ways to make it stick—and have a lot of fun in the process. To that end, we've created this seven-session group discussion guide. Most people feel this is just about the right length for a group series. Though we've created this discussion guide for group use, it is also adaptable for individual couple's study if you and your partner prefer to go through the questions on your own or are unable to connect with others who are studying the same curriculum.

Before your group meetings, it would be helpful for you to read the assigned chapters associated with the session, but this is not required. Obviously, you are going to get more out of the discussion if you've "done your homework." So if you can make the time to read the chapters, great! If not, don't worry. You can still join in on the discussion (it doesn't rely on having read the chapters), and you don't need to feel an ounce of guilt. The purpose is to enjoy the interaction and to learn from it. You can always read the chapters later, if you wish.

Here's a quick glimpse at what you'll be doing in each group session. We've designed each session to last about an hour, but you can take more or less time as your schedule dictates.

Just for Fun (4 minutes)

Each session begins with a question or activity that is "just for fun"—a kind of icebreaker. These are just to get the wheels turning and to help you connect as you come together as a group.

DVD Notes (15–20 minutes)

In addition to hearing from Les and Leslie Parrott, each session will include two brief video segments featuring several real-life couples who are exploring these issues just as you are. As you watch the DVD, feel free to fill in the content points supplied, in addition to jotting down your notes, questions, and reactions in the space provided.

Exploring Your Workbook Exercise (15–20 minutes)

Each of the sessions will rely on an exercise from this workbook. You will typically spend time within the group session doing the exercise, then discussing it. While of course it would be helpful to have the exercises completed beforehand, you may do them within your group if you wish. We've selected exercises that will not put anyone on the spot or force anyone to share information they don't want to. Of course, your group may elect to use other exercises from this workbook to discuss if you wish. That's up to you and your group.

Time to Discuss (20 minutes)

The list of questions you'll find in this section is designed to spark ideas, reactions, and real-life examples. As you interact, remember that a key ingredient to successful group discussion is vulnerability. This doesn't mean you have to say anything you don't want to. It's just that, typically, the more transparent you are, the more meaningful the experience will be, and the more open others will be as well. Vulnerability begets vulnerability. However, we caution you not to use this time to gripe about your partner in some way. Don't embarrass each other by dragging out dirty laundry you know would upset your partner. You want to be genuine and vulnerable, but not at the expense of your partner's feelings.

Another key ingredient in these discussions is specificity. You'll gain much more out of this time when you use specific examples with each other. So with this in mind, we will remind you to "be specific" every so often.

Finally, if you are a group facilitator, don't feel that you need to follow the order given or even use every question. Let the dynamics of the discussion be your guide.

Taking Time as a Couple

Finally, we've included suggestions for ways you can take this group experience into your week together as a couple. We encourage you to further discuss and apply the material as a way to connect and grow together. And of course you can also read the book together or individually if you can make the time. Again, no pressure or guilt.

One more thing: Relax. Have fun. And enjoy the opportunity to master life skills that will improve your relationship and help you develop a strong foundation for a marriage that will last a lifetime.

Have You Faced the Myths of Marriage with Honesty?

*What you believe about marriage will become
the fuel for your behavior in marriage.
For this reason, exploring the myths of marriage is essential.*

Just for Fun (4 minutes)

Whether you are doing this as an individual couple or as a small group of couples, take a moment to name one of the most romantic movies you've ever seen. It could be *Sleepless in Seattle, Casablanca, Titanic, Jerry Maguire, Father of the Bride, When Harry Met Sally*, or any of the hundreds of other romantic stories. What makes this movie so romantic to you? Do you see yourself in it? From your perspective, what's the primary message of the movie? If you don't like this line of questioning, name a romantic movie that you didn't like. Why?

_____

_____

_____

_____

DVD Segment #1 Notes (13 minutes)

• Your beliefs are the fuel for your behavior.

• Myth #1: _____

• Unspoken Rules

• Unconscious Roles

Exploring Your Workbook Exercise (20 minutes)

Within your small group, take time to complete exercise 2 in your workbook. This exercise explores making conscious your understanding of the roles both you and your partner have in a marriage. If you are comfortable, share with the group: What insights did you have while doing this exercise? How have your families of origin influenced your understanding of roles? What items did you have to renegotiate?

DVD Segment # 2 Notes (8 minutes)

- Myth #2:

- Myth #3:

- Myth #4:

- If you try to build intimacy with another person before getting whole on your own, all your relationships become an attempt to complete yourself.

- A-Frame Relationship =

- H-Frame Relationship =

- M-Frame Relationship =

Time to Discuss (20 minutes)

1. Which ideas expressed in the video were new to you?

2. Which concept talked about in today's session can you apply to your relationship?

3. In what areas of your life is your relationship operating as an A, H, or M?

4. What other myths do couples bring to the marriage relationship?

Taking Time as a Couple

To further explore marital myths you may have believed, spend some time this week as a couple reading chapter 1 and completing exercises 1, 3, 4, and 5 in the workbook. If you have time, also discuss the reflection questions with your partner.

Can You Identify Your Love Style?

Do you have a crystal clear concept of love?
And do you see it the same way as your partner? This session will ensure
that you get on the same page as you write your love story together.

Just for Fun (4 minutes)

Whether you are doing this as an individual couple or as a small group of couples, take a moment to answer these questions together: If you were designing a recipe for the perfect romantic day, and money wasn't an object, what would go into it and why? What would you do together to cultivate romance for twenty-four hours with an unlimited budget? As you reflect on this daydream, consider how romance relates to love. In other words, what percentage of married love do you think involves romance?

DVD Segment #1 Notes (7 minutes)

- Passion is the _____ component of love.

- Intimacy is the _____ component of love.

- Commitment is the _____ component of love.

Exploring Your Workbook Exercise (15 minutes)

Within your small group, take time to complete exercise 6 in your workbook. This exercise should help you define love in your own terms and compare your definition with your partner's. What qualities of love were most important to you? To your partner? Discuss with the group how your definition of love compared to your partner's.

DVD Segment #2 Notes (11 minutes)

• How to cultivate passion (for women): _____

• How to cultivate intimacy (for men): _____

• How to cultivate commitment (for both men and women):

_____

Time to Discuss (20 minutes)

1. Which idea presented in today's session did you find most interesting? Why?

_____

_____

_____

_____

_____

2. In your love life right now, which component of love seems most powerful: passion, intimacy, or commitment? Why?

_____

_____

_____

_____

3. In what ways can you nurture each component of love: passion, intimacy, and commitment?

_____

_____

_____

_____

4. Why is it important to remember that love is constantly changing and growing?

_____

_____

_____

_____

Taking Time as a Couple

In order to better understand your love style, spend some time this week as a couple reading chapter 2 and completing exercises 7, 8, and 9 in the workbook. If you have time, also discuss the reflection questions with your partner.

Session Three

Have You Developed
the Habit of Happiness?

*This habit can make or break a marriage. And it's important to remember
that it has little to do with your partner and everything to do with you.
In other words, an upbeat attitude is highly contagious.*

Just for Fun (4 minutes)

Whether you are doing this as an individual couple or as a small group
of couples, take a moment to answer these questions together: Consider a time when you had "one of those days"—a time when nothing
seemed to go as planned. Looking back on it, can you find any humor
in it? If your experience was written into a sitcom, what would the
name of the show be called and why? Now, think about how you typically respond when unexpected circumstances interrupt your plans.
Anything you'd like to change about your attitude in these times?

DVD Segment #1 Notes (9 minutes)

- The one habit that can make or break your relationship is the

  capacity to _____.

Exploring Your Workbook Exercise (15 minutes)

Within your group, complete exercise 10 in your workbook. Share with others how you see your attitude shaping the moods of your marriage. What types of things affect your mood? What negative self-talk have you used, and how can you help your partner avoid negative self-talk that she might use?

DVD Segment #2 Notes (7 minutes)

- The 3 toxins that can seep into a marriage relationship:

_____

_____

_____

- The most important quality of a marriageable person is

_____.

Time to Discuss (20 minutes)

1. What struck you most about today's session?

_____

_____

_____

_____

2. When are you most likely to blame your partner?

_____

_____

_____

_____

3. Do you think the most important quality of a marriageable person is the habit of happiness? Why or why not?

_____

_____

_____

_____

4. What keeps you from *choosing* to be happy?

_____

_____

_____

_____

Taking Time as a Couple

To further explore how your attitudes can affect your marriage, spend some time this week as a couple reading chapter 3 and completing exercises 11 and 12 in the workbook. If you have time, also discuss the reflection questions with your partner.

Can You Say What You Mean and Understand What You Hear?

Communication is the lifeline of every marriage. But too often the lines of communication between couples get crossed. Rest assured that this session will help you speak each other's language fluently.

Just for Fun (4 minutes)

If you are doing this as a small group of couples, take a moment to play the "whisper" game. One of you begins by whispering something (at least three sentences long) — it can be about anything (what you had for lunch, what you like to do on vacation, your idea of a dream wedding) — and the task is to convey the message around the entire group. You can't ask a person to repeat the message. You simply have to whisper to the next person what you heard. You'll be surprised by how the message ends up. If you are doing this session as an individual couple, talk about a time when you encountered a major miscommunication. What happened?

DVD Segment #1 Notes (10 minutes)

• Men _____ talk

• Women _____ talk

• Communication Basics

- Skill #1: _____

Exploring Your Workbook Exercise (15 minutes)

Within your small group, complete exercise 13 in your workbook. Compare your score with your partner's and discuss how well each of you is communicating. If you are comfortable, share with your group areas in which you can improve your communication.

DVD Segment #2 Notes (7 minutes)

- Communication Basics

- Skill #2: _____

- Without being genuine, the best communication techniques in the world will fall flat.

Time to Discuss (20 minutes)

1. Which ideas presented in today's session were new to you?

_____

_____

_____

_____

_____

2. Which concept presented in this session seems most difficult for you to put into practice?

_____

_____

_____

_____

3. Empathy involves using your head *and* your heart. Which do you tend to use more—your head or your heart? How can you begin to cultivate using both in your interactions with your partner?

_____

_____

_____

_____

4. When do you feel most understood? When do you feel least understood? In what ways can you better communicate your own feelings about being understood?

_____

_____

_____

_____

_____

Taking Time as a Couple

To learn more about successful communication in your marriage, spend some time this week as a couple reading chapter 4 and completing exercises 14 and 15 in the workbook. If you have time, also discuss the reflection questions with your partner.

Have You Bridged the Gender Gap?

Everybody knows that men and women are different. But what most newlywed couples don't realize, until they cross the proverbial threshold, is just how pronounced that difference is. This session will help make that transition much easier.

Just for Fun (10 minutes)

If you are studying this curriculum with other couples, divide into two groups: men in one group and women in another. In each group, appoint a facilitator and a secretary. Answer the question, "What do you want the other gender to know about your gender?" What insights do you gain from hearing what the other group has to say? If you and your partner are completing this on your own, discuss the same question with each other.

_____

_____

_____

_____

DVD Segment #1 Notes (11 minutes)

- How men and women solve problems:

- Men want to _____ it.

- Women want to _____ it.

Exploring Your Workbook Exercise (20 minutes)

Within your group, complete exercise 17. This exercise should help you communicate your deepest needs to your partner. Share with the group the needs that were most important to you. How did these needs compare with those of your partner? How do you see your needs changing as you grow in your marriage?

DVD Segment #2 Notes (7 minutes)

• Men need _____ _____.

• Women need to be _____.

Time to Discuss (15 minutes)

1. What ideas did you hear today that were new to you?

_____

_____

_____

_____

_____

2. What general gender differences have you experienced in your relationship?

_____

_____

_____

_____

_____

3. How can these gender differences cause conflict in your marriage?

_____

_____

_____

_____

_____

4. What steps can you take to celebrate the differences you both bring to your marriage?

_____

_____

_____

_____

_____

Taking Time as a Couple

To further explore how gender differences affect your marriage, spend some time this week as a couple reading chapter 5 and completing exercise 16 in the workbook. If you have time, also discuss the reflection questions with your partner.

Do You Know How to Fight a Good Fight?

*Conflict is inevitable. No matter how "in love" a couple is,
friction eventually emerges. But the savvy couple knows how to use
this conflict to their advantage. This session will show you how.*

Just for Fun (4 minutes)

Sometimes people fight about the silliest things—like an insignificant detail in a story they are telling, how someone is driving the car, etc. What's the craziest conflict you have ever heard of and why? Also, have you ever encountered a conflict because you were convinced you were right about something and it turned out you weren't? If so, are you willing to share it?

_____

_____

_____

_____

DVD Segment #1 Notes (12 minutes)

• Negative feelings that get buried have a high rate of resurrection.

Exploring Your Workbook Exercise (15 minutes)

Within your group, complete exercise 21 in the workbook. The skills learned from this exercise should help you and your partner avoid needless conflicts by remaining emotionally open with one another. If you are comfortable, share with the group how you felt when sharing withholds with your partner.

DVD Segment #2 Notes (8 minutes)

- What to avoid in conflict:

_____

_____

_____

_____

- XYZ Formula: In situation X, when you do Y, I feel Z.
- A great way to turn a _____

  into a _____

Time to Discuss (20 minutes)

1. What causes the biggest conflicts in your relationship?

_____

_____

_____

_____

_____

2. How do you usually handle conflict?

_____

_____

_____

_____

3. As you were growing up, how did your family typically handle conflict? What habits have you taken with you into your adult life?

_____

_____

_____

_____

4. What "conflict habits" have you brought to your new relationship?

_____

_____

_____

_____

Taking Time as a Couple

To further explore how to handle conflict in your marriage, spend some time this week as a couple reading chapter 6 and completing exercises 18, 19, and 20 in the workbook. If you have time, also discuss the reflection questions with your partner.

Are You and Your Partner Soul Mates?

You can do everything right in marriage and still wake up one morning and wonder, "Is this it?" You will continually be looking for depth and meaning in your relationship until you explore your spiritual nature — how the two of you walk together with God. This session will show you how to do just that.

Just for Fun (4 minutes)

Research shows that married couples who pray together enjoy a better sex life. What do you think of that? Why do you think this is so? And what does it say to you about the spiritual aspect of a married couple's life together?

_____

_____

_____

_____

DVD Segment #1 Notes (6 minutes)

• On a scale of 1 – 10, most churchgoing couples rate the importance of spiritual intimacy as a 9 or 10, yet rate the level of satisfaction with their spiritual intimacy as a 2 or 3.

• Couples who pray together report higher satisfaction with their sex lives.

Exploring Your Workbook Exercise (15 minutes)

Within your group, complete exercise 23 in your workbook. This exercise explores reaching out to others as a way to strengthen your marriage. What are some activities you and your partner came up with to serve others? How do you think this service will impact your marriage?

DVD Segment #2 Notes (8 minutes)

- When it comes to cultivating spiritual intimacy together, every couple has their own unique style.

Time to Discuss (20 minutes)

1. On a scale of 1 to 10, how important is spiritual intimacy in your marriage? Explain your answer.

2. On that same scale of 1 to 10, how satisfied are you with your current level of spiritual intimacy? Explain your answer.

_____

_____

_____

_____

_____

3. What are you presently doing in the area of shared service?

_____

_____

_____

_____

_____

4. What is one thing you can do as a couple to strengthen the spiritual aspect of your relationship?

_____

_____

_____

_____

_____

Taking Time as a Couple

To further explore the spiritual nature of your marriage, spend some time this week as a couple reading chapter 7 and completing exercises 22 and 24 in the workbook. If you have time, also discuss the reflection questions with your partner.

Saving Your Marriage Before It Starts

Seven Questions to Ask Before—and After—You Marry

Drs. Les and Leslie Parrott

A trusted marriage resource for engaged and newlywed couples is now expanded and updated.

With more than 500,000 copies in print, *Saving Your Marriage Before It Starts* has become the gold standard for helping today's engaged and newlywed couples build a solid foundation for lifelong love. Trusted relationship experts Drs. Les and Leslie Parrott offer seven time-tested questions to help couples debunk the myths of marriage, bridge the gender gap, fight a good fight, and join their spirits for a rock-solid marriage.

This expanded and updated edition of *Saving Your Marriage Before It Starts* has been honed by ten years of feedback, professional experience, research, and insight, making this tried-and-true resource better than ever. Specifically designed to meet the needs of today's couples, this book equips readers for a lifelong marriage before it even starts.

The men's and women's workbooks include self-tests and exercises sure to bring about personal insight and help you apply what you learn. The seven-session DVD features the Parrotts' lively presentation as well as real-life couples, making this a tool you can use "right out of the box." Two additional sessions for second marriages are also included. The unabridged audio CD is read by the authors.

The Curriculum Kit includes DVD with Leader's Guide, hardcover book, workbooks for men and women, and *Saving Your Second Marriage Before It Starts* workbooks for men and women. All components, except for DVD, are also sold separately.

Curriculum Kit   0-310-27180-0

Also Available:

0-310-26210-0	Saving Your Marriage Before It Starts	Audio CD, Unabridged
0-310-26565-7	Saving Your Marriage Before It Starts Workbook for Men	Softcover
0-310-26564-9	Saving Your Marriage Before It Starts Workbook for Women	Softcover
0-310-27585-7	Saving Your Second Marriage Before It Starts Workbook for Women	Softcover
0-310-27584-9	Saving Your Second Marriage Before It Starts Workbook for Men	Softcover

Your Time-Starved Marriage
How to Stay Connected at the Speed of Life

Drs. Les and Leslie Parrott

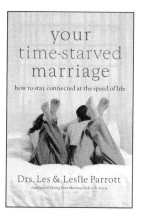

This is not a book about being more productive —it's a book about being more connected as a couple. In *Your Time-Starved Marriage*, Drs. Les and Leslie Parrott show how you can create a more fulfilling relationship with time—and with each other.

The moments you miss together are gone forever. Irreplaceable. And yet, until now, there has not been a single book for couples on how to better manage and reclaim this priceless resource. The Parrotts show you how to take back the time you've been missing together—and maximize the moments you already have. *Your Time-Starved Marriage* shows you how to

- relate to time in a new way as a couple
- understand the two lies every time-starved couple so easily believes
- slay the "busyness" giant that threatens your relationship
- integrate your time-style with a step-by-step approach that helps you make more time together
- stop the "time bandits" that steal your minutes
- maximize mealtime, money time, and leisure time
- reclaim all the free time you've been throwing away

Learn to manage your time together more than it manages you. Dramatically improve your ability to reclaim the moments you've been missing. *Your Time-Starved Marriage* gives you tools to feed your time-starved relationship, allowing you to maximize the moments you have together and enjoy them more.

Hardcover, Jacketed   0-310-24597-4

Also Available:

0-310-81053-1	Time Together	Hardcover, Jacketed
0-310-26885-0	Your Time-Starved Marriage	Audio CD, Unabridged
0-310-27103-7	Your Time-Starved Marriage Groupware DVD	DVD
0-310-27155-X	Your Time-Starved Marriage Workbook for Men	Softcover
0-310-26729-3	Your Time-Starved Marriage Workbook for Women	Softcover

Love Talk

Speak Each Other's Language Like You Never Have Before

Drs. Les and Leslie Parrott

A breakthrough discovery in communication for transforming love relationships.

Over and over, couples consistently name "improved communication" as the greatest need in their relationships. *Love Talk*—by acclaimed relationship experts Drs. Les and Leslie Parrott—is a deep yet simple plan full of new insights that will revolutionize communication in love relationships.

The first steps to improving this single most important factor in any marriage or love relationship are to identify your fear factors and determine your personal communication styles, and then learn how the two of you can best interact. In this no-nonsense book, "psychobabble" is translated into easy-to-understand language that clearly teaches you what you need to do—and not do—for speaking each other's language like you never have before.

Love Talk includes:

- The Love Talk Indicator, a free personalized online assessment (a $30.00 value) to help you determine your unique talk style
- The Secret to Emotional Connection
- Charts and sample conversations
- The most important conversation you'll ever have
- A short course on Communication 101
- Appendix on Practical Help for the "Silent Partner"

Two softcover "his and hers" workbooks are full of lively exercises and enlightening self-tests that help couples apply what they are learning about communication directly to their relationships.

Hardcover, Jacketed   0-310-24596-6

I Love You More

How Everyday Problems Can Strengthen Your Marriage

Drs. Les and Leslie Parrott

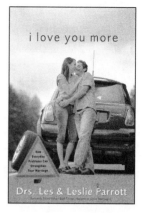

How to make the thorns in your marriage come up roses.

The big and little annoyances in your marriage are actually opportunities to deepen your love for each other. Relationship experts and award-winning authors Les and Leslie Parrott believe that your personal quirks and differences—where you squeeze the toothpaste tube, how you handle money—can actually help draw you together provided you handle them correctly.

Turn your marriage's prickly issues into opportunities to love each other more as you learn how to

- build intimacy while respecting personal space
- tap the power of a positive marriage attitude
- replace boredom with fun, irritability with patience, busyness with time together, debt with a team approach to your finances … and much, much more.

Plus—get an inside look at the very soul of your marriage, and how connecting with God can connect you to each other in ways you never dreamed.

Softcover   0-310-25738-7

Also Available:
0-310-26582-7	I Love You More Curriculum Kit	DVD
0-310-26275-5	I Love You More Workbook for Men	Softcover
0-310-26276-3	I Love You More Workbook for Women	Softcover

Pick up a copy today at your favorite bookstore!

ZONDERVAN®

GRAND RAPIDS, MICHIGAN 49530 USA

WWW.ZONDERVAN.COM

We want to hear from you. Please send your comments about this book to us in care of zreview@zondervan.com. Thank you.

ZONDERVAN®

GRAND RAPIDS, MICHIGAN 49530 USA

ZONDERVAN.COM/
AUTHOR**TRACKER**